The Boys on the Corner

Scenes From Another Land

The Boys on the Corner

Scenes From Another Land

John Holt

**The New
Atlantian Library**

THE NEW ATLANTIAN LIBRARY
is an imprint of
ABSOLUTELY AMAZING eBOOKS

Published by Whiz Bang LLC, 926 Truman Avenue, Key West, Florida 33040, USA.

The Boys on the Corner copyright © 2017 by John Holt. Electronic compilation/ paperback edition copyright © 2017 by Whiz Bang LLC.

All rights reserved. No part of this book may be reproduced, scanned, or transmitted in any form or by any means, electronic or mechanical, including photocopying, recording, or any information storage and retrieval system, without permission in writing from the publisher. Please do not participate in or encourage piracy of copyrighted materials in violation of the author's rights. Purchase only authorized ebook editions.

This is a work of fiction. Names, characters, places, and incidents either are the product of the author's imagination or are used fictitiously, and any resemblance to actual persons, living or dead, businesses, companies, events, or locales is entirely coincidental. While the author has made every effort to provide accurate information at the time of publication, neither the publisher nor the author assumes any responsibility for errors, or for changes that occur after publication. Further, the publisher does not have any control over and does not assume any responsibility for author or third-party websites or their contents. How the ebook displays on a given reader is beyond the publisher's control.

For information contact:
Publisher@AbsolutelyAmazingEbooks.com

ISBN-13: 978-1945772757 (The New Atlantian Library)
ISBN-10: 1945772751

For Kerwin and Meyer

...and his yelling rose into an indignant lament as he waved his arms more wildly, and hopped wildly into the air at every few steps, in an access of terror.

- Paul Bowles from the short story *A Distant Episode*

The Boys on the Corner

Scenes From Another Land

brown bag

standing around watching the traffic
shine in the slowly setting sun, hot orange, big globe
shooting the breeze about Stanton's homeruns,
what a dumb ass Trump is, that Hannity cat on TV is
    some kind of jerk,
see that nice one moving across the street, but she
    don't want my ragged ass
the boys on the corner dance the ephemeral surreal
    two step
they haven't worked in years, have no need to, really,
    none at all
unless you count the laundry, answering phones,
    staying alive gigs
in the state prison, you know doing a nickel here, a
    dime there
and now they're up to what they've always done so
    well
getting by, getting high, smoking straights, passing a
    bottle
closing in on five and a spliff of Jamaican magically
    appears smoothing the ride
as they pool a few wrinkled bills, some change, a bus
    token, how'd that get here?
enough cash always seems to be around somehow
hustling, dealing a little, stashed, family, lift a wallet,
    hot items
one of them hoofs it around the corner, be right back,
for a few pints of Beam
at Mickey's Liquors, good prices, no shit about bad
    habits
booze on the cuff when times are slim, owner not an
    outsider,
living good, the high life tonight in midsummer form

The Boys on the Corner

chicks walking past working it with skimpy clothes on
    in this heat
and with the whiskey comes five quart cans of Black
    Cat ice cold
like we said, the owner's cool, he understands, he's
    okay,
a couple of fresh packs of smokes, a handful of Garcia
    y Vega
cops leaving this block alone chasing crack uptown
so a man can enjoy his liquor, his freedom standing
    out here
under a street light sharing whatever all this is with
    his friends
the buzz is easy, talk is casual, sliding around hard
    times lived, survived
the boys are doing what they do best
killing time on planet earth

pawn

that's all any of us really are
little pieces moved around a twisted, collectively
    imagined board
doing the bloody work for the corporate thieves
that run what's left of this world
hell, they own presidents, senators, countries
what chance do any of us have in all this sickness,
    darkness?
but the boys, all five of them,
hanging out on the street
know this better than most
one of them got kicked
out of college and he's white
another got in and he's black
and, of course, good at football,
but got booted out because
they didn't dig his arrogant attitude
and the others have had their share of
bounces, routs, busts, repos, divorces
Remember that Grand Prix…one fine automobile
Too bad you missed the busters on that one
you name it, they don't fit in
are unable to play the upscale game
that's required to make the bucks
granting entrance into the phony
buying the illusion of class, no breeding club
with two homes, expensive cars, portfolios
trash talk from low class losers
running from their own insecurities,
all of them, the five of them, standing right over there
    laughing
at a bus that just ran over newspaper vending
    machines, brakes shot,

The Boys on the Corner

would rather stay a little, maybe a lot, drunk, high
out of sight, invisible, out to lunch
they can't hack, stand, tolerate the plastic hustle
current society, generous word, shoves
down our throats, the one way too many of us buy
without lives, souls, hearts, energy, friendships
these guys would rather swipe a car stereo
spin the machine off for a few bucks
at DeBois Pawn, checks cashed here,
then blow the money at Mickey's

on Scotch, smokes, cigars, Slim Jims,
maybe Snickers or Sneekroes as they call them
they're broke, dead end, bound for not much of
    anything
but like they say midway through the second pint
    that's going down easy
Man, we ain't nobody's fuckin' pawn
we're just who we are

jive

That's one ugly dog you're walking there, sport
Oh my mistake, that's your women
Didn't mean anything by it, cool down
Forget that gun, hold the knife
and the four stand behind their friend, all of them
    laughing pretty good now
because she had trashed them hard over the years
because they drank too much, were lazy, no good on
    the rack
now her latest sucker looked the other way, stashed
    weapons, kept on walking
he didn't want any part of the boys in their present
    state
whiskey, beer, a little wine, desoxyn, reefer, an
    attitude
that said what the hell, bring it on
Christ! She's mean but not bad for a dog
No wonder you're divorced, man,
Can't talk about women like that not even among
    friends
That's not acceptable, no way, no way
Fuck off! And here comes that lame ass cop Farrell
    again
who pulls up to the curb, to their corner, gets out,
    walks over, so cool, tough guy
gives them the once over, starts a spiel on public
    drunkenness
that maybe he'll run their useless asses in, starts to
    call for backup
but before he gets to this an older lady with grey hair
    in braids to her waist,
pushing a grocery cart holding everything she owns –
ratty sweaters, paper bags, Styrofoam cups, a black
    dial phone (for emergencies only)

The Boys on the Corner

a stuffed puppy, broken Barbie dolls, old lottery
    tickets,
Converse hightops without soles, half-full jug of
    Paisano,
a few old paperbacks like Blood Sport, Wamba, Where
    Paradise Lay,
envelope with divorce decree (1968), commitment
    papers (1969), release papers (1982)
the old girl slams her cart into the side of Farrell's
    squad car, and again and again
over and over as she mutters I didn't vote for the
    cheap ass sucker,
the son-of-a-bitch belongs on Venus not down here
    with us decent folks
and she backs up a few feet and really lets 'er rip
    crumpling the door panel,
knocking off the sideview mirror, shooting broken
    Barbies onto
Farrell's squad car front seat on top of his clip board
the boys are cruising now passing the brown bag
    bottle around
lighting smokes, puffing on cigars, offering sage
    advice
Give her hell, Farrell, run her ass in, not ours, she's
    real trouble, shoot her
call for backup, SWAT team, ATF, hoopy-toopy-ten-
    four sucker
and they know they caught a slight break with
    Mandy's, that's her name, craziness
so they stroll back around the corner, slightly past
    Mickey's Liquors, into an alley
full of garbage, passed out drunks, hookers making a
    few bucks up against brick walls

John Holt

towards the back of the filthy cul-de-sac to a rusting
    fire escape where they do four flights to the top of
    a tenement, then they climb an iron ladder to the
    roof, straight up where they've got chairs, shaky
    tables, a chaise with no legs, a radio with good
    batteries
they settle in, line up the bottles, plenty for tonight,
    set out the smokes, cigars
turn on the game, Cubs-Cards, Lester versus
    Wainwright, 4-1 bottom of the third
Schwarber went long bases full, it's a warm evening, a
    few stars fight through the dirty sky
all of them are home now, a joint makes the rounds as
    Baez doubles off the wall
Sheeit, that Mandy girl is one crazy bitch, but she
    saved our ass again
damn cops think she's really out there, they won't bust
    her, just run her
down to the Mission where she was headed anyway,
    yeah she's nuts alright
Russell singles in Javy, crowd through radio going
    nuts at Wrigley
that last book she wrote, what's her damn name on
    that one, Natalie something,
the one called Hunted in Paradise about those crazy
    western dudes, ranchers, whatever the hell,
made her a lot of money, movie rights I hear, we got
    to buy her something
for saving our asses all the time, 'cept she's got more
    money than all of us together we'll ever get our
    hands in this ragged ass life, saw her safety deposit
    box last year before Christmas, packed with
    hundreds, crisp bills, too, gave me five of 'em, one
    for each of us,
remember? pass me the whisky, not the Scotch, the
    Beam and toss me a smoke,

The Boys on the Corner

Yeah we got to do right by her someday, we sure do
And the Cubs are winning in style just like the five of
   them this forgiving night

junk

they knew about this one, been around with it some,
do a little number with death, see how close you come,
snort a few flakes, smoke the shit with a little Oaxacan
spike in the arm long running for two of them
not a good situation, any port in the horrific storm,
when they were younger and still believed in the con
the one where if you played it straight, worked hard
had some big time dreams, aspirations
well, hell, of course you'd succeed in the world
but the young fucks who did the business college
    number
the ones with no morals, values, scruples
who lived for the back stab and the illusion of power
they thought money created, well, damn, those
    bastards
ran the boys over like they were long-dead, rotting
    road kill
the sorry ass money changer fools road, ride around
    in their BMWs,
travel where they're told its hip only to be seen in self
    mirrors
own houses in the best of places, bulky portfolios, all
    set they are, you bet,
disappointment strikes deep with those holding
vision, talent, drive and most of all hope for all of us,
maybe most of this can be clicked to a brighter
    channel if we think big,
that's what some of us believed, still believe, the boys
    being part of this
benign, insane, egalitarian aristocracy of the air
    waves,
booze always works, but when you're hurting hard
you try anything looking for escape from the hell

The Boys on the Corner

that comes from the first awful recognition that we're
    a failed experiment
in the most horrible, macabre, grotesque, bizarre of
    ways
so the boys on this dreamland corner disappeared
during their somewhat misspent, misshapen youth
    hammering the needle
ripped on acid, mescaline, STP, MMDA, mushrooms,
    peyote, opium,
morphine (they all liked this sister), Demerol, brown
    Peruvian flake
and of course heroin, the number that nearly finished
    off three of them
but God intervenes in strange ways, there were things
    for them to do here, to accomplish
maybe it was nothing more than giving cop Farrell
    shit, or
fading a drink and a joint to the girls working nearby
    or
merely putting in the slowed down, hard time called
    living
or perhaps there was something crazy, mysterious,
    important
coming round the corner someday down the strange
    road, who knew, knows?
so they all walked, crawled, screamed, writhed,
    sweated, shook their way free

from the hard stuff and settled in for the ride with
    booze and reefer
their lives were garbage, trash, worthless in the eyes of
    the pathetic money chasers
like they could give a damn
they knew junk when they saw it

dead end

the guy had a ticket on the oblivion express
turned state's evidence
big time meth setup
most of them wanted
him dead
weird people, shaggy characters
barely neighborhood fits
walked passed his hotel all the time now
murderers
undercover stiffs
trying to keep him breathing
to make their case
a real sad scene
all these cats chasing down
their righteous perversions
the boys laughed a worked on
a bottle of Johnnie Walker Blue
one of them had lifted
from an uptown store last night
not bad, but then booze was booze
the wanted soul traded heroin for methadone
a cheap trick of sorts
what did he care
dead is going to be dead
and he's already there
when the trial date came
he sang his tired song
then went to prison
for some time
and managed to survive
some serious debasement
now he's out
no one goes near him though
he's a soon dead man
always was

outsiders

they come down here in taxis
or leave their Lexus, Porsche
somewhere safe downtown
make the walk in safe numbers
to the rougher side of things
drugs, unemployment, sex,
pawn shops, liquor stores,
flop houses $8 per week no key,
seedy bars with package goods,
gunfire in the background
setting up the hot night,
cops just not around,
a forgotten community
of society's casualties
living harder than the
recently rich ever saw as they
slum the afternoon away
getting cheap laughs gawking
like soul sucking ghouls
at the downtrodden riff raff
the trash society forgot to take out
Oh my god! Look at that one
he's peeing in the alley
and that one's passed out
in that pile of garbage
will you look at the outfit
that whore's wearing
pink, green and purple
and all that makeup
who'd sleep with her
out in public like that
and the three husbands
the pussy-whipped arbitrageurs
dragged along for the ego ride

John Holt

are thinking that they'd all like
a piece of that pink, green and purple
who would no doubt at least
move in bed and not do
the corpse hideous on her back
like their wives pretend once a week,

while the boys drifting away on a
Saturday afternoon dreamland
express coach look on at
the affluent half dozen
losers who are trying to casually
stroll away their fear, nerves, guilt
but they aren't succeeding
and everybody moving through, along
Callender Street knows this
the silent wave laughing
builds with experienced joy
then one of them
wags one finger
remaining silent
slaps the tourist
with open hand
offers drink of whiskey
while the outsiders, unaware
that their own little used radar
is picking up on
derision, teaching, cognition
grow tight, talk brittle
eyes darting scanning the
foreign scene that would
easily accept them if they
had an inkling about living, humility
but the pricey community
children are clueless
you folks lost, need a drink

The Boys on the Corner

the bottle of Beam is offered
the women scurry off
like frightened fish
as do two of the trained husbands
the third slows, turns
takes the bottle, doesn't wipe the neck
looks at the boys drinks deeply,
takes a breath, drinks again
hands the pint back
says thanks, with a look
that acknowledges the bs
he's trailing along with
Anytime, man, come on back
we'll be here all the time
don't have any big plans
that we can recall this instant
all of them laugh, eyes dancing
the boys and the one
from the far outside
for just a few moments
float the white light river
as one person, as equals

ever upward

perhaps they don't exist
but I saw one sitting on a bench
rotting, wrinkled, forgotten
the rainbow fantasy went belly up long ago
huddled in concrete
backs against a dead wind
lonely, depressed, ignored
victims of universal, internal terror
banging out the last moments on a crapped out
    machine
wealthy ones stare past the obvious
making high level (not Alberta) putrid moves
against all of them
evil, senile, loathsome
it's said that science extends life
all now can exist longer
what the hell for?

tired

most of the time they get a kick out of all of this
the mad masks and posturing that passes for
    personality
they'll maintain their enthusiasm for the ultimate joke
all of us struggle with in the day to day
one of them, the clown who was kicked out of
the creative writing program at Beloit College
long years ago in southern Wisconsin
still writes down his images, thoughts, feelings,
but there are those rare days that show up dark and
    miserable
where the five of them just don't have the juice
to joke away the pain, failure and disappointment
not even the whiskey helps or the pot
and they stand around like dying trees
unable to smile or see through the terror
just blowing about in the frightened breeze
grinding along through a real tough time,
that's when they realize that they are
just plain tired from all of it
and each of them utters
a silent, sad prayer
for the strength
to continue

empty machine

don't have money
doesn't matter
newspaper vending machine
opens without coins
free news
one of them fakes shoving in change
lifts the lid
no papers left inside
should of checked first
before making the small play
liquor store owner
offered sage advice
about looking before wasting the money
on dead issues
no paper today

newsprint

the premise is bogus
a perceived need to know
sellouts entrusted with the truth
idea pickpockets
distort life with daydream headlines
needless to look in honest mirrors
to earn a thief's paycheck
lies with a fake smile
personal plastic touches
feeding gigantic menace
paid for by dull minds
while those assembling the drivel
barely laugh anymore
the daily fix
a collective orgasm
of words, too much color, photos
twisted meal
banquet of perversion
served on double talk porcelain
children wasted by maniacs with .357s
jackals drool while taking notes
the truth is not part of the equation
keep rolling the stuff out
over and over
a pr pimp faking reality
deceit grows thick
pass the bottle
tell the lies
makes way
for tomorrow's fabrications
one day at a time
is barely bearable
so never let sanity
stand in the way
of an honest lie

the girls

strut their stuff down the street
with casual, well-practiced style
ostentatious flair
that soon appears subtle
way out in the middle
of all of the traffic
you know the
drunks, beggars, pimps
cops, hustlers, thugs
crack heads, junkies,
narcs, thieves
cabs, buses
Olds Cutlass Supremes,
squad cars, garbage trucks
the rogue Caddy
ambulance meat wagon gone crazy
chopper overhead
big jet higher yet,
all the junk, man
and the girls with their
sexy swagger
make the boys' days
worthwhile as they murder
hot pavement afternoons
smoking stale cigarette butts
swigging warm Tokay
fusil oil enhanced
and the eyes are
bloodshot, yellowed
worn out some
but they clear and brighten
as the tits and asses
bright eyes
work their rolling thunder

The Boys on the Corner

magic on weathered bodies
that stand a bit taller
a little straighter
dignity slight flashing
joy faint shining

when the sashay ladies
beam those electric smiles
at the five of them who are
now thinking that maybe the day
ain't so bad after all
'cause of those damn girls

weather

hard to cheat this one
when money goes mainline
for booze, reefer, smokes
there's little financial room to move
inside to The Zoo Gardens
for a few shooters or score a flop
when rain, snow, heat
whips down the street
so the boys hide
beneath alley overhangs
or slide in
to that empty warehouse
down by the river -
brown water filled with filth
and dead fish
a body or two in season
and when the almighty hawk
rips and tears howling
around corners and through
threadbare clothes
a couple of burn barrels
Proulx toxic waste books
smoldering away within –
rags, yesterday' papers, wood skids -
the abandoned business
along with maybe a boosted
bottle of Beam from Mickey's
and a pack of Camel straights
works well between mandatory
dining excursions at the mission
standard fare – beef noodle soup, bread, jello -
not much but it's free
and the stuff 's base for the booze
most of the time the weather

The Boys on the Corner

sizzles, freezes or drips bone chill mean
but come a few weeks in spring
or perhaps early fall
everything is sweet
and the park works for spacing

but this is uncommon decency
and the boys often say
"can't do nothin' 'bout this stuff"
as they look up at the yellow smog sky
and they pass the bottle
round once again
shivering against a winter wind
crashing down from mountains north of town
or seek shade when the heat
blasts in from the high plains
on a dusty breeze that's as dry
as they are standing out there
broke, thirsty, fighting
the weather

grinding it out

pushing through an ugly day
hell, any day
is tougher than the boys
make it look
sleeping in the warehouse
or in the park under bushes
or in the alley beyond The Owl bar
wrapped in old newspapers
all five of them
waking at dawn with the shakes
and oh so thirsty
dry like water never knew
the bottle saved already gone
among the five of them
when a siren roused them
at three in the wind and fog
now they count seconds
until Mickey's opens at seven
for breakfast – white port, Camels, Snickers
then off to hustle, steal, beg, borrow
the day's dough for booze, reefer, ice, cigs
breakfast at 7:30
dining graciously at the
Mission bar and grill
powdered eggs, powdered juice, dry toast
then the slow glide slightly up in spirit
on the wine, scoring some whiskey brown bag style
ride the visuals of human flotsam on the streets
when a book is discovered discarded in a trash can –
Vollmann's *Rainbow Stories*
they take turns mouthing the loony words
all of the tales strange
about goofy jive like
scintillant orange, yellow sugar

The Boys on the Corner

blue yonder, violet hair
the boys couldn't make the words
as they read aloud like
thespians on a concrete stage
but then, Vollmann never knew
what he was about either
so an afternoon died this way
until cocktail hour, more whiskey
fresh smokes and an uncommon treat
small bag of mescaline passed off
by a freak on his way south
on the run to New Mexico
the boys saved his ass
hiding him from a bust
repaid the favor in special currency
buzzing good as evening settles in
with over twenty bucks between them
soft around the edges
cool glow on the fringe
no shakes now, no worries
grab an extra pint for the morning
and they do knowing
damn well that the sucker
will never see the sun rise
but once again
like the down and out busted
pros they are, eternally will be
they ground another one down
worked the bastard into timeless dust
one less day to fight for or through
maybe the next tune brings
the unspoken wish
the dream that is weightless peace
an end to hell here on the corner
the number called "Death"

night

neon

heart of the night
starts beating early
like a jazz-crazed demon
on the run hard time
from previous destinations,
where doing the required
demanded of all
killing brings to life
latent anger within
a listless flock
starts long ago time shuffle
when the natural light fades
behind the western ridge
of busted teeth mountains that shine
hot pink, burnt orange
buzzed turquoise, crazed chartreuse
electric yellow, flame red
false gold, bright white
wasted spectrum
all nighttime luminaries
showing off their
shining reflections
bouncing up from the
oily puddles
left by recent
casual thunderstorms
casting surreal honest
glowing shadings
reminiscent of artificial rainbows
on the boys as they hang lazily out
on the corner by

The Boys on the Corner

The Turtle Tap
at Montana and Central
where all the traffic
hooks on by
long legged, tight assed
big breasts, thick makeup
for twenty bucks
in a quarter hour
less if you've got the juice
fired by attractive brilliance
blazing, flashing, winking
above bars, pawns, drug stores, flops
manmade rainbows
artificial radiance
refracting too, too
truthfully abstract failures
committed by those who
tried and failed
arcing and wrapping
around disappointments
enticing and carousing
all night through

landscapes

streets greasy, hot, cracked
skid marked, littered
sidewalks dirty, gum-stuck, cigarette butts, spit
soiled condums
fake dollar bill flyers
pimping strip shows swirling in the wind
alleys filthy, dumpsters stinking,
trash bags ripped open
putrid, dead or alive

John Holt

bodies stinking
cats, rats, mongrels, humans
buildings old, crumbling, soot covered
window cracked, decrepit
ghost faces behind stained glass
sky washed out blue turned
smog yellow, brown grey
nighttime washed out
in atmosphere crud
no stars, moon, galaxies, planets
flop house old man
behind counter
in front of keys
ratty couches, black-white TV
candy machine empty
cigarette machine busted
ancient Hustler, Time, Sports Illustrated
crapped out events
from long ago no time
Harry Crews
Scar Lover
on butt burned table
thread bare carpet
overflowing ashtrays
cigar stubs, gum wrappers, toothpicks
rooms stink, urine, sweat
defeat, despair, death
wash stand, bed lice, head lice
stained sheets, pillowless
bare dried out wood floor
no curtains, bare lightbulb
steam radiator heat
yelling, screaming, snoring
loud radios, murmurs
sleep turned pastime
a distant dream

The Boys on the Corner

hallway closet toilet flushing
like bomb going off
through rattling pipes
shattered mirror
stained yellow and rust sink
shower drips is all
tile floor muddied, bloodied
walls creaking as bricks
cool contract,
heat expand
payphone in hallway
no one to call

dreams

from that other
real world
where homes
families
a twisted sense of security
reside beneath
manicured lawns
some fantasy remains
with the bounds
of disillusion
but being way beyond
the ability to dream
to even remember
what these are
while still knowing
they exist
the awareness
causes them pain
when they see

John Holt

this hopelessness
in the eyes of the
innocents

cruisers

they come from where
there's a little money
disingenuously gathered
selling nothing on computer
byways jazzed with
sick electrons
moving numbers
manipulating accounts
screwing everyone they see
or can imagine
especially mirrored images
of their ghastly selves
walking dead
feeding in parasitic suburbs
driving pricey cars
like BMW, Mercedes, Lexus
Hummer, Yukon, Esplanade
looking for pieces of ass,
the kind they're
afraid of back home
and will never have anyway
the oldest son's best friend
already has his rough
hands on this stuff,
action maybe laced with
cracked smoke
silver flasked single malt
and the ladies know

The Boys on the Corner

the hustle, work it well
for all it's worth
that twenty bucks and a chance
to ride the murder glide
driven by psychotic dysfunctionals
in pricey clothes and even more
expensive, analyzed personalities
out to kill the real life flourishing in
the boys' neighborhood
they do this with overpriced hate
the monied losers do, cruise for
blow jobs, drugs, adventure
and that ultimate voyage
even down this way
where death doesn't rate
top billing anymore
lost that tag a million
too deep hangovers
suicides, ODs, shootings ago
but the outsider mad clowns roam
attempting to kill and yet
like whatever they touch
the long-gone-dead
hanging tight to existences
that are way beyond alive
far past suburban alienations

cops

not many of them mean well
thugs, psychotics, sociopaths
small minds, envious
big mouths masking
insecurity building

John Holt

egos run riot
riding herd on the streets
pigs directing humans
like a fascist nightmare
in war-torn Watts
on the take, running the con
unemployable outside the force
they thunder along
in their squad cars
fully loaded, literally
high on what they bust
looking for trouble that rarely exists
except in officious, confused minds
that have long gone mad
scanning prey that only
wants to exist alone
without official intervention
or societal meddling
but cuffs, pepper spray,
night sticks, gunfire, tasers
perpetual harassment
are all part of the drill
ask the boys about all this
rousted, beaten, shot at
busted for vagrancy
intoxication, theft, possession
big time beef in squint eyes
questioned about this
threatened about that
all of the usual suspects
and the cops know
that what they're doing
improves nothing
clogs the system
and more to the point
fuels a blue boy paycheck

The Boys on the Corner

that isn't measured in money
and does nobody no good
fires less than latent urges
to put the screws to those
who wander slightly lost
on all the wrong sides
of these exhausted, hell hound
streets

terror

what's a little
stark, raving
abject fear, horror
bugged-eyed madness
when the last thirty years
have been riddled,
shot up the ass
into the veins
China white style
for the foolish
sake of running from
the clown ghouls
that gobble the brain
feast on the soul
while lunatics in DC
bomb the hell out of
anyone who disagrees
has oil, isn't white
drives a camel
worships Allah,
or the criminally dead
tap into what's
left of privacy these times,

John Holt

so screaming silently
through an internal night
that mocks you forever
with a sick grin
a sardonic laugh
that echoes like
rabid bats bouncing
off skull bones,
and is little more
than a sad man's
dying attempts at
trying to remain sane,
then even terror
has its purpose

sensibilities

cooling asphalt
like kerosene
gagging a
cool wind
auto exhaust
chokes, burns
grain alcohol
slices air
stale booze on
empty stomachs
puke, hunger
dissipation
roaring buses
car horns
ripping ears, minds
hip-hop-gansta -rap-crap
feeding hate, frustration

The Boys on the Corner

cleaning dough
transmissions slipping
through worn metal
like fried joints
screeching tires
string through a can
rough scrape of
shoes on concrete
rasping like dead grass
within drought plains
moving within hot, dry wind
white port, Tokay
sickly sweet on the tongue
tasting of saccharine corn candy
tears mixing with dirt
on worn out clothes
back to bad booze, defeat
filth, resignation
ambulance, cop sirens
all show no hope
swirling about with
mangled authority
whores scream over territory
like down-on-their-luck
politicians
hand on light pole
warm metal, rough grime
all blending in a vision
that spins in washed-out color
through drunk eyes
external seasons of the
lost, sad, judged

rats

John Holt

rodents creep out
with animal caution
like the vermin they are
far too close to a subspecies human
that brokers lives for wealth
at the cost of their souls
and the end of others' dreamscape
as light dims to stealth
hours pass and drunks
guzzle, stumble, pass out, are beaten
in alleys scarcely lit by
dim service entrance bulbs
and rats big as terriers
move in with yellow
razor-sharp fangs
gnawing on dissipated flesh
clinging to unconscious bones
that never feel the creatures
ripping and tearing muscle
in bloody chunks that
drip from ghastly jaws
dead is already dead
in a lifeless epiphany
piercing, glowing eyes
scan the scene for
predatory intrusion
none around so
human life is torn from
temporal pavement
as rat existence flourishes
in a black heart landscape

The Boys on the Corner

      violent

this one's a jester of sorts
not quite what it may seem
cause it isn't about rape
woman, child nor man
in the insane blackness
nor screaming crazy in the middle of traffic
nor knifings or beatings in dim lounges
nor taking out somebody's windshield beneath a
  streetlight
not related to yelling, screaming, swearing in dark
  rooms
mutilating and consuming
organs like chamber music
trapped within a macabre recital
nor flashing the bird
nor hate, anger, disgust
this one's about the
relentless, insidious
never forgetting wastings
of human dreams
women, money, recognition
or the real juice –
peace, serenity, belief –
dreams that lead
inside human souls
the boys carry the pain of this atrocious
long-running humiliation, destruction -
all of them smart
though not as much as before,
consumption takes a toll
the booze plays hard here,
all of them caring if
only a little bit these days -
that's where the liquor, drugs

chain-smoking comes into play
what's a little death trip
when you've already been
beaten senseless for decades

greed

why'd you make an issue
out of the estate, man
one of them asked the other
hot day, warm whiskey
rolled smokes
spliffs, bali shag
nothing afternoon
what's new?
thought money was
the way of it
wanted the old Caddy, too
and her ring
no mind for
anybody else
only me wanting things
more so than
family, friendship
arrogant attorney
helped me grab
all the wealth
did manage to
cost myself dearly
guilt driven
extravagance
new car
good booze, bad results
clean drugs, dirty habit

The Boys on the Corner

sharp women, sliced heart
nice joint in the wrong place
all of the crap and more
that kills wisdom
brings us always back for more
over and over
alive, dead, alive, dead
greed takes its toll
wasted everything of value
to meet up with hell

                      loss

all of them
have experienced
the going away
that never returns
departings of all sorts
divorces, fights, emancipations, driftngs
one's mother dropped dead
while making her
nightly old fashioned
swizzle stick
still in hand
smile of shock on her face
quick and clean
another lost a daughter
years back
heroin spiked
somewhere in Alaska
dead end state
with bs attitude
calling themselves tough
but only weaklings

John Holt

hiding from
themselves
lost inside
ex-wife called
let him know
he was worthless
hung up
never saying
when the burial
would be
where it was
so he always
carries the wonder of it all
carved in his scarred heart
how cruelty
becomes perceived virtue
and if perhaps
there are flowers on
her grave
on any grave

death

the body
is lying just
up in the alley
the remains have been
lying there for
more than a day now
splayed form
arms legs akimbo
holes in soles
of shoes
cloths filthy, ragged

The Boys on the Corner

bottle of Muscatel in one
grimy hand
clutched like
a drowning man
clinging to a
sodden piece of wood
trash already piling up
like windrows
against the corpse
flies buzzing
the heat makes
things smell like
the living dead
have come for
a visit on the corner
one of them
decides that he's
had enough
tells the others so
walks into Mickey's liquors
calls the cops
and comes back out to wait
a few hours later
a squad shows
figuring what's
one more dead drunk
rags over noses, mouths
they check out the stiff
call for an ambulance
wait for the arrival
oversee the loading of
the dead man
drive off and
everything is back
to normal
men drinking, smoking

John Holt

hookers hooking
pimps hustling
junkies nodding
death on this street
is nothing
nothing at all

big c

none of the boys will talk about it
they all know the demon is waiting
maybe already found them
through windows of cigarettes, booze, drugs
dead end living
the big c scares the hell out of all of them
they each know someone who's died
of the shit recently, in the past, now
coughing lungs out in bloody foam
withered into skeletons
morbid skin stretched skulls
yellowed. sunken eyes
a friend of their's
used to be big money
until he picked a fight with booze
would stroll up to them
smoking a meerschaum pipe
drunk, broke, still cocky
in an understandable way
and say "that fucking cancer won't do this old bird"
the boys would lean away from him
one making the sign of the cross
another muttering "save me from this fool"
and they'd change the subject
if the pipe smoker persisted
they'd ice him out

The Boys on the Corner

pretend he didn't exist
wasn't there
one day last week he wasn't
bone cancer wailing out of
commonplace nowhere hell
now
he's dead
they don't like
the big c

dharma

dharma for one
Ian Anderson once blew
with no awareness
no success
complete understanding
while vainly talking reality
grasping at buddha teachings
form, sensation
perception, memory
consciousness
form, no form, form
not really close
mind empty
gone, gone, really gone
totally, completely gone
perhaps little more than
bicameral dreams
genetic predispositions
pretending visions
Skandha aware
that is not space
emptiness that

John Holt

is not emptiness
look for a river
find the river
again no river
in flood stage
white jade whipped
smashed black dragon pearls
avoiding increased flaws
then the always outsiders ask
without knowing
what is
what is not
receiving answers
still uninformed
cold moon
high wind
no horizon
speechless, silent
their response
forms emptiness
lonely is bad
being hurt worse
giving pain to others hell
so the boys dig deep
for a change
discovering
just enough
for another bottle
that appears full
but is not empty

blood

on the tracks
under the bridge

The Boys on the Corner

spreading, thickening
feeding flies, ants
as it cooks
on the hot
pavement where
the boys look
and see a knife
throat stuck
in an old drunk
with filthy-pants pockets
turned out for cash
a squad car rolls by
two brush-cut pigs
look then laugh
with hellish obscenity
mouths jammed with
chewed food
they glance again
before turning back to
crimson-jellied doughnuts
black coffee
dark like dead blood
that smells of
counterfeit copper
the boys knew the man
no one living here
is a stranger
they watch the squad car
fade in morning traffic
before placing a bottle
half full of bourbon
in the dead guy's hand and
shove a little money back
in his pockets
a short funeral of sorts
their small caring

John Holt

as they think, know
that this is just one
gruesome, grisly
street that dead ends
around the world

gifts

once a month out of the blue
on the first day
under the counter
at Mickey's Liquors
a box of Siglo IV's
$100 bill inside
two packages of gold toe socks
waiting for him
he knew who they were from
but had forgotten the name.
sharing the cigars lasted a week
and the money bought the booze
for the same seven days
he shared all of it
with the others
and they got to wear new socks
each month
feet washed under a spigot
in the alley behind Mickey's
one time a Taj Mahal album
appeared with the other stuff
Oh So Good n' Blue
he didn't have a pillow
so he broke the records in half
in the albums cover
then halved again

The Boys on the Corner

with hands, feet and a knee
now he had a place
to rest his head

                        revival

lord have mercy
on our ragged souls
the energized preacher
intoned
arms stretched
like heron legs
gangly, perhaps gaunt
to a smog yellow sky
traffic roaring past
the true gods of
modern life
yeah verily like
clockwork
every afternoon
around two or so
the grey haired old man
would appear as if
by biblical magic
old testament?
in front of the boys
wearing a black robe
white starched collar
    military spit shined
    coal black shoes
    black beret
    gold cross earrings
    always intoning
    the same old, no sense

John Holt

    words about
    redemption
    salvation
    eternal glory in heaven
    free at last from
    the burden of life
    they'd listen
    and smoke
    and drink
    and one of them would go for more wine
    and smokes
    and the preacher would scream
   "Amen!"
    and the boys would whisper
    amen

                    angels
the true beauty
is difficult to hide
walking on by
floating slightly above
the hot, cracked sidewalk
impossible to describe
when a true women
the one who sees all of you
and with a wise grin
flashed your way on waves
of pure thought
shows you that you're
worth getting to know
worth helping along the crazy road
because she says we,
all of crazy us we,
truly belong in the

The Boys on the Corner

white light river paradise
that flows way beyond eternity
lasting for a forever second
and if she really goes on a roll
she'll move next to, inside of
you, your soul
and the boys have been blessed
with this rarest of experiences
each one of them
at least one safe time
creating
memories that linger
flourish
nourish
help
keep
them
alive

end game

comes on fast
the ever-popular
brain fade two-step
rides in on a very high horse
nostrils flared, foam-flecked lips, cracked teeth
when the hour shifts to off
dream landscape ghouls dance
pudding thick, drying
blood crazy
on rubber bones
knees turned weak
cadaver ligaments can't hold on
the brain wanders from view

John Holt

except for skewed vistas
from insane hell
that always lusts unfulfilled
then blacks out
one or two of the boys
a touch less gone
help the others to wherever
safety hides like a stalking cat
in this relentless scene
they've had enough for this day
doing nothing within emptiness
being perceived as even less
requires one hell of a lot
of energy, stamina, guts
when checking out
often makes more sense
so the inevitable shift to
a quiet place of invisibility
those who know don't remember
warehouse, park, alley, abandoned car
ubiquitous dumpster
warmed with paper, food scraps,
cardboard boxes torn up
or maybe if things play well
up on their roof top hideout
if they can crawl that high
fire escape leans out from
corroded bolts sticking out
from rotten brick
no Mary Deare wrecks
around here in
this parched far country
naked land
soaked in gold
foundered
run aground again

The Boys on the Corner

then only then
rising on high tide
before agonized
breaking to pieces
to sink among
jagged rock islands
like mangled bones
no, these are definitely
the gentlest of touchdowns
though still called crash
when the dead of night
takes over

death visits the cancer ward

a lot of things not to like here
look at reporters on tv
they're nuts
so are the ones in the cars pretending to drive
buying groceries turned dangerous game
one bastard no one likes in the least
always killing ones that love, care
with no offer of even fake hope
strange sleight of hand when
simple mistakes like smoking, drinking, eating
wind up costing the ultimate in steep priceyness
and some of them don't do a thing
still dead just the same
this trip needs lots of refinement
crap that doesn't belong here
never give in to the twisted son of a bitch

post time

one of them remembers,
the one raised around sports and the trappings of a
    privileged birth,
the days of American Sportsman
cape buffalo in Africa, trout in Ketchum
partridge and pheasants far out in the Dakotas
way back on ABC TV,
back when networks championed quality
instead of marketing scams devised by
young punk ad execs with no life skills,
with Bing Crosby and Phil Harris
and another batch of boys –
hunting, fishing, drinking buddies -
similar in many oblique ways to the boys on this corner
    today
raising hell all around the place
fishing for sea run browns in Tierra del Fuego
lion hunting in Kenya
dove shooting in Mexico
tarpon fishing off of Boca Grande
tracking Faro sheep in the Yukon
ancient lake trout in Great Slave
and at the end of every day
as a wild landscape sun touched down
there were the drinks and
Phil Harris raising his tumbler high
saying "post time" with the joy of a real drinker,
the one of the boys who remembers tells the story to the
    others
they all nod and think that this is one hell of a way to travel
so they sally forth to the Socialite Club
stroll in with great aplomb, panache,
a certain air most commonly associated with those of regal
    birth rights

The Boys on the Corner

after all they have twenty-eight bucks and change between
    them
a twenty found along the curb hiding among the litter of
cigarette butts, gum wrappers, hand bills for strip shows,
and eight crumpled, wadded dollar bills retrieved from
    well-worn pockets
along with spent matches, bits of tobacco, a Gerber knife,
they order as one entity
"triple bourbons on the rocks for each of us"
the bartender looks at them with curiosity
they are assured, happy, confident
an unusual occurrence along this hard-time part of down
where the cool wind blowing down from high country
is normally knocked senseless by desert furnace action
before this breeze, gale, tornadic gust shoots down streets,
    around corners
whipping up dirt, dust, paper, making life a little tougher
    than it needs to be
"and one for yourself, buddy"
when the drinks arrive they all raise them eagerly,
the bartender getting right with this one,
laugh and smile at each other and then at the grinning
    bartender
and with the best of Phil Harris in a neighborhood he'd
    never visit
they say firmly with the rare power of recognition that they
    too are hunters
of a peculiar sort, and more importantly,
men who stay with it hard times or not
so they say as one
"post time"

dt blues

haze is real
so is the room
madman spinning flirtations with death
awful confrontations
with sick truth
nothing is comfortable
except the pain
thirty stumble getting here
dreams gone bad
loving turned ugly
whiskey the only truth
in a dishonest scene
out of the way now
'cause he's comin'
through
guns and all
some think they can help
talk and sincerity in measured steps
an old time medicine show
can't fill the void left
by a departed companion
cerebral circle jerks
in smoky rooms
don't cut it
and the haze is real
killed someone who got him here
fixations replacing placebos
madness dancing on
an un-dug grave
damn real and
much clearer now

straight

get a load of that clown
can't believe that sucker
spoiled brats and check-out lines
spirituality is some trip
everything looks strange now
all of it the same
really doesn't seem any different
neon light confusion
whacko back there
rough flight to here
air is still choppy
imagined promise isn't visible
staggering in liquor's own time
tripping, lying, screaming
grab the rail
say tilt
windy bitch storm
on the horizon
tossed out a window
into unknown territory
blasted by brightness
scraped bloody raw
by the facts
these I don't recall
who the hell are they
this is not home
never been to Disneyland before
moving on fast step
need some blurred vision
spin, spin, babble and blubber
somewhere recognized for hiding
screw responsibility
want the friend back
the one who kills with the swig

John Holt

so what damnit
these guys are killing with their eyes
just another con
misery loves the miserable
this straight-up number
isn't all it's cracked up to be
so long

motion

keeping at it all the time
with a quick shuffle
makes as much sense
as other stuff
the boys own today
sometimes clarity
trips into the movement
scary but feels good
too bad it is
temporary in nature
when making do with battery acid
juicing through veins
passes for living
the current jumps starts stops
that cannot be the rhythm
they're born with
not lurching
not sneaking
wail fearless
dance spinning on one foot
mad gleam
all hell fearless
the band is union
and will not play long

urban sprawled

sliding across the plain
used to be dark out at night
road still straight
one hundred miles an hour
accepted behavior
moonlight mystery
wild emptiness
never needs filling
is smothered
in neon avalanche
highline glows bleakly
prairie Vegas
full of losers
crapped out
on dead dreams
the boys know the routine
have been down the dusty two track
looking for visions that are
ghostly mirage
scenarios that zip, zoom, fly away
in febrile mind heat
and that magic
dirt road is hard to find
cautious navigation
scares up
friendly desolation
rare places unseen
connected
by undefined space
miles up
looking down
not much darkness
growing glare

epidemic

scattered all over
valleys mountains deserts
large groups
sickly herds
the great dream
offered out west
never meant for this
junk a metaphor
raped spirit
dying pockets
hope freedom
buried by weight
mindless existence
boom bust transience
cities, towns
visual dumps
skeletal remains
soon to be
scraped away
by distant ice

coming home

one of them
leaning against
the lamppost
heart song remembered
a highway glowing
in moonlight
inside instruments
soft green light
Allman Brothers
Hot 'Lanta
Jim Beam
plenty of it
sat nearby
Camel straights
on the dash
going fast
road traveled before
earlier
poured a pitcher
on game playing
woman who
liked morons
wanted to screw
her father
tall pines cast shadows
on small lakes
silver reflections
valley surrounded
by mountains
the river flows
in cold night
cigarettes burn down

John Holt

whiskey is smooth
keep going faster
heading north
plenty for back when

cold

broken off like dead twigs
snapped in a mean breeze
piled up against
a rotting fence
frozen wind crawls
over empty hands
dirty white with frost
lifeless weeds
shake in
barren wasted territory
tough lightless
surviving brutal miles
filled with nothing
dragging up a hard path
ears fill with ice
skin hardens
cracks
falls away
scratch claws on door
of dead dreams
that glow silver
that are merely
total darkness
hiding from the cold

feelin' alright

they start the day very early
way before normal people get out of bed
feeling a lot like dead
the beast demands attention
with the booze pulling away
like a train going to hell
and ripping out wired nerves
along the blood rusted tracks
wicked stuff when you live on it
depend on the not quite false promises
the liquor offers and grants
in its own demon ways
that are often blacked out
or forgotten in the stream of
never-ending drunks
day after day
year after year
so they shuffle over to Mickey's
already open for the morning
got-the-shakes bunch
that lines up before city traffic begins its workout
they slide along a wall to keep from falling over
feet never leaving the filthy pavement
too damn tired to lift legs and there's
always the fear of falling fast to the hard surface
moving with a graveyard shuffling sound
like dry wheat blowing against itself
in a lifeless wind down from the nearby mountains
and they grab some wine and a pint and some beer
holding the stuff with both hands
so they don't drop it
in a foaming, sweet stinking mess
on the brown-yellow linoleum floor
digging the money out

The Boys on the Corner

that they somehow managed to save from the night
    before
getting it across the counter
to Dominic who passes back some change
is a rattling, stuttering bitch
outside they slip into one of their alleys
open the beer in a yeasty mist,

twist the metal screw caps on the cheap grape
pour the liquids home as fast as they can
they pass the bottles around
and finish the beer and the wine
so by the time they're on to the whiskey
they're starting to feel pretty good once again
like the day holds promise of god knows what
they start laughing quietly and share smiles
that say we'll get through this mother
this son-of-a-bitch that never offers us what we
think we want, deserve and need
'cause we're feelin' alright now

insane

you could probably have
queried Bukowski on this one
perhaps *Crucifix in a Deathhand* style
or *Notes of a Dirty Old Man*
or maybe *Ask the Dust*
of Fante on a
passably good day
and Steinbeck wandering along
Tortilla Flat and *Cannery Row*
(not Hemingway though, he's scared stiff)
they know
we know
but most
won't admit to this
the simple truth
a hat hanger that
proudly, regally states
we're all fucking crazy
crazier than true hell
burning electric orange
nuclear fusion hot
inside all of our
little pea brains
as we pretend oh so hard
to be straight arrows
in a tight-ass society
ruled by mind-dead
political puppets
whose strings are pulled
by entities that make
big oil look like
Tinker Toys
in a plastic playground
and these small fools

The Boys on the Corner

pompous in their
TV pronouncements
bob and weave
like poor actors
on bad acid as they
jerk and wrench the
filthy strings
that we've allowed
these zero time jerks
the obscene right
of hooking through
our torn hearts
our own private though
interwoven roads
to psychic ruin
all the way down
wondering, wailing
confused, frantic
anxious, panicked
yeah, all the way down to hell
screaming madly
we're not insane...

plain crazy

out where it's empty
wind talks
rain is an uncommon friend
there are some strange people
blown away
by the electric hum of nothing
running small stores
growing weeds in the dust
real drunk
linked together
by the white light express
that ties all of us
in a twisted knot
mountains blast out of nowhere
screaming in the sky
large creatures wander fearless
disrupting the current
with their curious buzz
snow and ice sweep down
cattle freeze
minds vanish
the beating moves in constant time
and is hard to disguise
the boys know
the way to travel
to here or there
the trick to this
is to skip off to oblivion
and enjoy the view

dancing nowhere

the great American pastime
crashing head on
where the front is obvious
not running down buffalo
not looking for images in ice water
or wandering
after scapegoat seasons
a lot of green thunderbirds
discarded and smashed
along dusty roadsides
dead men gasping
with whitewashed education
draining from torn ears
could not bank on truth
reservations were not honored
around chinookville
hometown for some of us
sliding along
on fusel oil
and ancient dreams
kicked aside
by forgotten collisions
with rotted pickups
the breeze drinks it all
bone dry

long time running

God the wonders keep coming
living in some of the best of it all
fools obsess with playground insecurity
nothing of importance
like shutting down a chainsaw
or sending an elected fool home
to read ag reports on local radio
and kiss ass for dough
with extraction industry yahoos
cultivated while back east,
or maybe positing a lame dialectic by
blowing apart an oil pump jack

oh no, none of that silliness

we got us here a bunch of clowns
who think they're big-time artistes
who think it's so cool, so hip
to slum it down in the boys part of town
with unfinished brick wall studios
and tacky galleries hanging crap
pretending to be art or drinking
in the local taverns to be part of
the real down to the dirt scene
and they want all of us to know
how long they've been around
pretending they're all real high plains cool
upwards of twenty-five years one of them
smirks with hooked beak upturned
while he dashes off pricey
faded color assembly line scenery
that the way-too-rich snap up
like hungry browns during hopper time
another, a mind parasite

The Boys on the Corner

steals others thoughts
turns them into crappy novels
while living off the generosity of others

the boys know these ones
and a few others
and in humorous anger
happily punch them out
every chance they are offered

yeah and I got drunk with Brautigan says one
spineless pretender
and I passed out in a gutter in '87 brags another

this is big-time stuff
ranking right up there
with grade school turf wars
playing cowboys and Indians
or giving each other cute nicknames like
captain c and tommy the turk
who really looks like a
dyspeptic Major Hoople on Everclear
which loosely translates into
raging insecurities manifesting
themselves as little kids

yeah and I lived in Missoula more than thirty years
     ago
says one of the boys, the one who studied about
being a real hot shit literary writer in college
a billions lives back there

when that town was a town
and not an overrun madhouse
that has nothing to do with Montana
back when the spring kegger of Oly and laced acid

John Holt

and no one knew Rock Creek, Bitterroot, Clark Fork
    tunes
Lost Highway, Mission Mountain Wood, The Top Hat
midnight runs on the Circus pinball machine at
    Eddie's
mescaline and champagne trips to Squaw Tit Peak

and I hung out in Whitefish when it was still a
    mountain town says another
the boy who used to sell stocks, securities, electronic
    frauds
Norton Buffalo, Swift Creek, The Palace, The Viking
one golf course, no gated communities, no Hummers
instead of a yupster-second-home-ski-crazed-golf-
    course-raped
hell hole that I no longer remember

so the fuck what?
we all are to blame for the goodbye to the best of it
me as much or more than most
whether we've hung around for thirty-five years, a
    hundred or a summer
nowhere time scales vindicating insecurity
no value, nowhere, at no time

but really, none of this silliness

necessary costumes required
black bandanas, Bowie knives, full camo
riding a psycho violence threat
to buy a little deserved space
from a long-dead now cold war
that can't be dropped
while terrorizing effete and fragile
wandering sidewalk fare
that can use the scaring

The Boys on the Corner

but all the same;
or silly hats and other affectations
because man I been on the scene
yeah all those artistes
figured this one out early on
fake the talent and run the con
mooches buy damn near anything

mountain, river, prairie
ponderosa, sage, prickly pear
wind, sun, rain
seasons, years, eons
grayling, cutthroats, bull trout
grizzly, coyote, elk
meadowlark, red tail, magpie
space, freedom, sanity

we're all way too hip
for all this natural silliness

guaranteed

banging down the hallway
mindless concern
ice hands turn that one
nothing in there
empty bottles
dead houseplants
old magazines
dusty sunlight
wasted novel clutched in hand
bloody knife in the other
ahead a crease of light
stains worn carpet
Wilco cuts the air
wine laughter unreal
who cares
could be fun
cat scratches soundless wallpaper
door swings
in cool draft of a crazy window
lots of people here
no place to go
no way to get there
cat sleeps on a drunk lap
stairway door blasted
off dull brass hinges
steps with no railing lead
to recognized garbage that is
the only way down
to an empty street

the way it always was

time jags
not a lot of change
a bunch of noise
living in the back
old crumbling porch
the clown across the road
hammers new high rises
filled with secondhand crap
masquerading as style
drinking cheap wine
being twenty
seems possible
though
up front counts
where's money success acceptance
old mountains ask
cutthroats fin beneath shadowy banks
laughing in fish talk
another language unknown
gibberish spoken here
at least hangovers
feel right for the boys
images shimmer wander and roll
but retain crystal clarity
faces scream by
madder than hell
aware of conditions
motion lags behind thought
in these them those
pleasant situations
one day chases another
pretty much the same
wrapped in different years
variations on a theme
worn ragged

3 a.m.

sitting up takes guts
all kinds of wild stuff
flying around
just below the ceiling
contact madness
reinforces uncertainty
that dims nicely
in morning light
private emotions
are rare commodities
at this hour
with quiet maniacs
on the loose
no time now for glamour
they stay low
play it straight

alley life

being completely nuts really helps here
when you're being run down
by a buffalo wolf and other dreams
and the only sounds you hear
are claws tearing concrete or
wind ripping through the wires
as an aging stoned whore looks down
from her third story window and
if she's kind she'll toss a potted plant
your way while the wild hound closes in
for a kill that can't get any worse
until some fool's radio blasts
the BeeGees' Staying Alive

the mint

every high plains town's got one of these
and this version is no better or worse
than all the others around the state
somewhat dark, dully neon
long wooden bar, mirror back
jukebox, gaming machines
pool table, booths
open early, closed late
the usual stuff
drawing the expected crowd
of local hard-core slammers,
including the five of them
when they ain't lounging on the corner
who pass mornings,
afternoons, evenings
years, lives
drinking draughts, shots
shooters, red beers
smoking steady strings
of cigarettes
talking about all of it
day after day
rain or shine
wind or snow or both
the place smells of booze
drunkenness, some happiness
a lot of disappointment
traces of loss
tragedy
every town's got one
killed my share of time
in most of them

small town, tiny cops

we all know the kind
crisp uniform, dark blue in this case,
shiny black leather belt, black holster hiding 9mm
    Glock, black shoes
that creak and groan as they approach
little radio-speaker job on his shoulder that squawks
    like a demented parrot
on loan from Jimmy Buffett
and the badge shines as does the name plate of this
    clown
who lives to play tough guy for no reason,
local jerk off in high school, now legalized bully
that maybe harasses the boys when they're way down
    on their luck
a little bit drunk, a little unwashed, a little broke
or pulls over an old rancher whose
muffler's shot and the engine smokes scorched oil
while local punks who the young cop
off duty drinks with, fucks their girlfriends, smokes
    their dope,
roar past in jacked-up trucks that blare
bullshit gangsta rap written for inner city blacks
with no heed, awareness of these dumb-ass high
    plains
white bread zeroes, but our blue man
waves at the wasted youth
as he cheerfully writes the old boy a ticket
ruining his day in town sipping whiskey, playing
    poker with friends
or maybe this officer of the law – protect and serve the
    jive hustle goes –
comes banging on some hapless bastard's front door
    while he's drinking Beam

John Holt

smoking cigars, listening to Coltrane as he writes this
and tells the guy with trumped authority that's
    pathetic funny
that if he doesn't start playing by the rules
he'll come back with a warrant and confiscate all the
    guns
and arrest him, send him to prison
take your best shot, sport, he says
go get that legal paper. I'll be here, and slams the door
    in his face
so he stands there until he sees an old woman walking
    her small dog
an animal that relieves itself next to a fire hydrant
and the cop runs down and tickets the terrified old gal
the writer can't watch so he turns up the music, heads
    to the kitchen and pours another drink

that's how we dance

you can go through the motions
kidding yourself all the while
that she means what she says
as you hold her on your way to the sun
but the ragged ass peaks generate
their own dark, wicked weather
so when you finally come down
from the illusion of a bright summit
and all those large trout are rising
on the deadly still surface of a dark lake
forget about a bright moon shining above
the harsh truth of her dishonesty

room service

old grey house
rented room
small with window
work out of reach
money always there
in right amount
champagne drunk
mescaline buzz
candlelight reefer
gold chain girl
snake head
around her waist
interesting
in twisted way
pills on dresser
need taking
returns late at night
from her rounds
high smiling
perhaps
not much
still plenty
for those
linked to
hot pavement

frosted

remembered often
unreal fantastic
avoiding such things
bubbly unconsciously
stayed all night
to catch up
became cloudy
too fast for sight
west of here
is pleasant
striving for good
with arms of car
sanguine legs of bourbon
warmed by violet leaf
recall initiates room
dark refreshed
with someone
who listens trusts
long dreary waiting
for them
not often sure
worth the risk
abject fear
of never realizing
causes damnedest
memoried hell

arrows – the boys soliloquy

oh the thoughtless things we do consistently
that pierce your sensitive, unique nature
and cause you such undeserved pain
when all you want is to love us,
or maybe anyone or anything
while living your expansive life of esoteric dimensions
that so few of us can comprehend.

but none of yourself is given
without the high cost of our emotional currency,
demanded with your gentle smile -
that hides a lifetime rage spawned from youthful pain-
the stuff we pay with, the wicked coin of your realm
that comes at dreadful prices, bargain basement
    games
revealing that nothing in your bleak domain is free.

you pass out a little kindness, consideration, passion,
never a whispered freedom, though,
with the arrogance of a tyrant, perhaps a despot,
and this rings the register with long-playing affairs
involving hack musicians, and oh-so-gay hairdressers
coupled with never-ending disappearing acts
through the snow to mommy's place
to hide out while she reaffirms our destruction,
and we continue to hope that some light
will make it through your dark eyes shine,
those are the dollars we pay with.

some good work together, unique vision
transformed into books, photos, articles, magic travels
resulted in positive influence
with money never and always an issue
and never ever was any of this magnificence enough,

The Boys on the Corner

forever with your vanishing acts while way out there,
perhaps in the book or perhaps out of the book
and oh the pain this life is causing you,
that you magnify and inflict and still
have the mad audacity to claim
that none of us can understand.

finally the price for your bleak pleasures
in this dark existence of your choosing, worshipping,
grew far too steep for us.
all this took was your moaning about
you're spiritual awareness,
and how our life together felt as if
your fragile emotions were being pierced with arrows,
drawing black blood we couldn't see
and for us the easy way out was getting drunk one
    bright day
and sending you down the road
was so damn easy,
an act we never imagined possible,
but so damned easy,
because we wanted some freedom back in our lives.

You bled us dry girl.

arrested development

this one confused the boys a good deal
when they first met her
thirty years long gone ago
not unusual with them,
because the fire seemed genuine
glowing from a soul
coming from a heart grown large
by hard living, enormous mistakes
and a lot of looking.
as usual they were wrong,
slightly addled, mistaken
and as always, learning slowly,
let alone believing that
another one never moved
beyond the playground,
instead, contentedly killing off the years
toying with, damaging the real.
abject terror grinding her soul
into bloody dust
remembered from childhood
schoolyard
games.

truth

the bottom line here
is that they don't have a clue
what any of you want
and most of you think
that they're only in it for the sex
or the control or the power
like all men you sometimes say
such is not the case
though the physical side of life
has its moments
but power, control, possession
they're for amateurs
too many hard times have been survived
too many hangovers weathered
too many loves blown away
too many disappointments faced
for that juvenile jive
and you all talk about easy friendship
while still being a man
whatever the hell that is
and then out of the blue
or perhaps the black
comes the fiery red wave
of intense rage
spawned by disappointment
with the inability to live up to,
satisfy, recognize or
walk the walk
then you are off to aldaville
claiming you need a sensitive guy
who is gentle, giving, understanding
and you really mean that you
need to exercise a bit of the crap

John Holt

you've just accused me of perpetuating
on some poor sap
until the hopeless boredom
circling these useless sycophants
drives you back to those such as us
who are head strong, focused
driven, opinionated
sometimes drunk, assholes
son-of-a-bitches, bastards
smoke 'em if you got 'em
always there as who they are
with no idea what's going down
what any of you want
how about being yourself
honest and just going for it
we'll head way up north
to the mountains and tundra
the ice blue skies
enormous rivers, the glaciers
and raise some hell
that's the truth

soft and lazy
(with thanks to Natalie Merchant)

their minds are soft and lazy
she sang with a bunch of maniacs
so many years ago
and like most other stuff she writes
she nailed this one on its dull head
but she's kinder than I
and suggests giving them what they want
they won't remember
where I would get in their heads
and insist that they be held
accountable for their
venalities, dishonesties,
their thoughtless behaviors
never give an inch on this one
but that's why she is who she is
and so many of us care for
her energetic, hopeful ideals
and I'm wandering the
high plains screaming
at an empty sky

arctic aurora

in a world gone mediocre
with television, sound bite blitz
and hack work politicians
gated golfing communities
people making too much money
doing absolutely nothing
of any value that I can see
insane wars, mad policy
strip mines, clearcuts, dams
with all this crap
look to the northern sky
watch the spiritual ghost dance
as unearthly colors
of radioactive elegance
shade, whisper, cavort
peach, azure, vermilion, emerald
shadowy luminescence
weaving within a backdrop
of universal objects
alchemy made real
the boys stand
and watch in awe
in reverent silence
as they gain bright visions
from lines of sight

not so bizarre going down

he is way gone
plugged into a 1959 Fender Strat,
one that good old Bogle
handled for the Ventures
Walk Don't Run, man,
tripped over the instrument
at some old lady's
lawn sale back west coast way,
and an old VOX Pathfinder
this cat is out there with the great alchemists
even by the boys arcane standards
reprising old riffs from The Seeds
while electrified and standing under a cold shower
the notes reverberating off
cracked, moldy tiles
muted by hard water
and none of them can figure out
why in the hell the kid,
call him Jeff Hoopy-toopy-ten-four
(his clandestine ID in
the state mental joint)
or he won't acknowledge your existence
let alone presence,
but the juice never phases him
all he says with a
Stevie Ray grimace
is got to run the electron fire
through the synapses
to do those boys justice
(otherwise I'm just another
skinny Mick Green
playing Pirates
and we don't need any more of those
ya know)

The Boys on the Corner

and he'll sail off into the
long ago esoteric garage band's
Up In Her Room
countermeasuring and freelancing
on the melody, loosely defined as such,
for hours, sometimes endlessly without the stops
the notes ripping and slicing out through
the open, busted plexiglass, shower door
through gaping windows
whose mangled openings
grin like freaks on STP
and then contrapuntally dripping
down onto the wired street
where the tones and tunes hitch rides uptown
on the Callender No.5 bus
packed with straights playing normal
idiot persona games,
you know the ones
CPAs, would-be maybe arbitrageurs
and all the rest of the lowdown
careerist flotsam that's
climbing nowhere but lower down the scale,
coming home from deadly jobs
bound for morbid suburbia
as Jeff Hoopy-toopy-ten-four's
electrocuted seed interpretations
find their way into the
squarest of cubicles in
manicured hedgerow hell
all the while the boys
lounge in the corner sun
drinking, smoking and laughing
as they watch the kid's music
oh so clearly visible
like freshly laundered nightmares
slide through the air determined

John Holt

to jack up some shot minds
that need a kick in the
cerebral ass
meanwhile back in the shower
our hero wages and raises holy hell
with the boogey electric
the water keeps running
the electricity keeps flowing
Hoopy-toopy-ten-four
over and far out beyond

inside angles

not much known
about the tallest
and maybe oldest of them
quiet, staredown eyes,
usually dead still
motionless,
even by the other four
despite the thousands
of down time
dead end hours
burned
while standing
slouching, shifting
on their corner
in front of Mickey's Liquors
Dubois Pawn – *Payroll Checks Cashed Here* -
The Turtle Tap
The Mint
all nearby
he keeps to himself
is called Ed
maybe fifty-five
maybe thirty
who the hell knows
the years make liars
of all of us
allow persona shifts
largely undetectable
even by stone wolves

spinning around
drive me nuts
like a bad advertising jingle
of Dean's *"this point in time"* doublespeak

The Boys on the Corner

always the damn images
of what might have been
an easy life in the mountains
away from the bs
fishing for cutthroat
working the ridges for spruce and blues
playing tag with grizzlies
walking with elk, moose
all that's lost now
and the loss
won't leave me in peace
won't give me a break
I killed her
she had it coming and
she knew it
betrayed my trust and love
with lust, drank me down
like cold beer on a
smoking July afternoon
the bottle dripping
icy condensation
screwed my best friend
was doing this
when I walked in
from that long day
fixing cable on lift five
at the mountain
a real bitch hanging
200 feet above the pines
peaks of Glacier
flashing white, purple
down east in the clouds
Cabinets glowing west
and they both laughed
when they saw that I saw
was shocked, wounded

John Holt

so I went to the truck
reached under the seat
grabbed the .357
shot him in the knees
her between the eyes
loud crashes, no sound
smell of gun powder ignited
haze of blue smoke
what a mess
blood, bone and brains
splattered all over the bed
windows, walls, rug
dogs scared as hell
ran away
someone down the road heard
called the cops
remember running through the aspens
limbs and leaves smelling green
slapping my face and hands
in the starlight dark
down to the hi-line tracks
timed my jump into a
Great Northern boxcar
froze my ass off
when it crested the divide
Marias Pass
cars creaking and lurching
over uneven rails
always remember the smell
of diesel exhaust
from those five Dash 9's
powering up the mountains
heard avalanches crashing,
whispering loud death
as tons of snow, ice, rock
sluiced over the wooden sheds

The Boys on the Corner

skipped in Havre
at the depot
scored a pint of Beam
at the liquor store
across the street
hitched a ride on US 2
with a trucker
then another down 16 to Sidney
and made it all the way to here
which is nowhere
I'd ever heard of
a place that maybe doesn't exist
out on the high plains
where sometimes I think
that my madness
can see clearly
from sea to shining sea
thank any God for these four
they don't ask
and I don't tell
we drink away the days
all of this hurts hard
but there's a little peace
now and then
enough so we can
catch our breath
and they're friends
trust like no other
we've got nothing else

and really none of them
are hip to all that much
about any of our past lives
doesn't matter, who cares
all of it is dead and gone
worthless, blown away

John Holt

like that gunsmoke
hanging out on the corner
where life is cheap
and getting high
drunk, stoned
is more a useful habit
that adds only a little
to the river light
they ride each day
maybe the one the other four
know so little about
was a big deal
back when
back where
none of them are interested
passing round the pint of Kessler's
smoking stale Chesterfields
taking it all in
as nothing at all
keeps on happening

acid rodeo

the first good day of spring
in the mountains
and they all got
ripped on acid
with whiskey chasers
here and there
rode the cross-town bus
out to the city limits
hitched from there in
the back of an old, rusted
Ford F250 pickup
to the dusty, weathered
rodeo grounds
some bands were playing at
the abandoned arena
and somehow
they got there
without hitting
any hallucinations
they each bought a pitcher
with money from a swell's picked wallet
the deed done yesterday at the corner
during rush hour crush
no one the wiser
and waded through the beer soaked dirt
a few cops
and thousands of people
tripping their brains out
under a clear sky
things turned crazy
as they always do
even the mountains
made a statement or so

The Boys on the Corner

just to keep things in perspective
the bands came and went
Mission Mountain Wood
pulled a hallucinogenic Lazarus gig
and played an extended set
that brought back real memories
before the group
faded like fog beneath a mean sun
and the crowd
was gone
the wind
up and blew away
it was wild
Doug Kershaw and topless women
and a bass player hit in the face
with a pitcher of Oly
never missing a beat
when the music stopped
they climbed in a pickup
for the ride back to town
four wheel drive this time
over the top of a Cadillac
roof crushed down
they kept going
to a bar
late and fluorescent bright
scrambled eggs and fried brains
shots of whiskey and
another rodeo down the drain

motion

keeping at it all the time
with a quick shuffle
makes as much sense
as other stuff
we own today
sometimes clarity
trips into the movement
scary but feels good
too bad it is
temporary in nature
when making do with battery acid
juicing through veins
passes for living
the current jumps starts stops
that cannot be the rhythm
we were born with
not lurching
not sneaking
wail fearless
dance spinning on one foot
mad gleam
all hell fearless
the band is union
and will not play long

epidemic

scattered all over
valleys mountains deserts
large groups
sickly herds
the great dream
offered out west
never meant for this
junk a metaphor
raped spirit
dying pockets
hope freedom
buried by weight
mindless existence
boom bust transience
visual dump
skeletal remains
scraped away
by distant ice

casting about

convincing the big boys to take
is even harder than they tell you
matching the hatch jive doesn't get it
nor does artful casting over classic water
with a dainty piece of pretentious fluff

the ones that matter, those worth the effort
will never buy the obvious con of this artifice

learning to see without looking
understanding how to chase without wanting
makes hammering an offering of substance
tight to a sweet lie just barely possible
with laughable stealth and silent humor

now damn it, why would anyone
want to do any of this to begin with

crazies

one of a kind, one of us, we are them, the boys say
in vehement, enthusiastic unison
the booze working good in them now
rising up northeast of town shoulder next to Sheep
    Mountain
a small band of outlaw mountains hiding out like
    many of us
an island range some call them
they climb thousands of feet
above the high plains
but seem happiest when the sky
is dead clear blue for dozens and dozens of miles all
    around them
yet their mad summits are obscured by dark, ragged
    sheets of swirling storm clouds
tiny creeks run down from the high country
eventually becoming streams with wild, native
    Yellowstone cutthroat trout in them
further down in the wide, open valleys rivers hold
    browns, rainbows, brookies, whitefish
this is what draws me to these isolated mountains
the aloofness, the trout, the strange weather, the lack
    of people, the high peaks
I'll walk off from old logging roads and catch trout the
    length of my index finger
and maybe see a grizzly or a wolf that biologists say
    aren't here
hard to argue with hard headed science, though
stands of old Ponderosa survivors rise thick-trunk,
    red-bark, banged up from
years of wind, cold, heat, drought, fire
on the north end of the lunacy lies the river and prime
    grassland

John Holt

to the east is an openness that measures itself in the
 earth's curvature
south past the Interstate and whizzing traffic stretch
 young mountains
west is still another stream of clarity then more
 straight-up peaks
right in the damn middle of all that's right about this
 place stand the Crazies
if only they'll let you really see them on a clear day

the man was blind

there's a blind man who lives around the corner
he's well-respected for all the right guilty reasons
but this doesn't keep him from being blind
and causing everyone in the area a lot of trouble
crossing a street is normally a four-car pile-up
yet he's won an award from some officious civic group
for being the most inspirational character in this part
    of town
the boys laugh at this one and know it means little if
    anything
even in this city of malevolence and mediocrity
the man barely stands out from all the others
he is adequate and that counts for something
in the midst of barely anything
but the clowns present the honor for the wrong
    reasons
the boys knew and joked about this over drinks and
    smokes
in the darkness of The Turtle Tap
they also knew that at times they weren't too bright
    either
see, the blind man bought a car for ten bucks
actually it was twenty but who's counting
an old rusted out Datsun wagon
it ran and the lights and turn signals worked
there was a rumor going around that
the wipers only wiped when the AM radio was on
the blind man gave the slick salesman a ten
actually a twenty but no one was counting
got in the car and drove home
one of the great mysteries in the boys' lives
on the way he picked his mother up at the foundry
everything was cool right until the end

The Boys on the Corner

as they pulled into the parking lot behind the
    tenement
the family dog, who liked to sleep on the warm
    pavement,
lifted his head to say hello to no effect
the blind man ran over the hound on his way to the
    parking spot
the boys and everyone else had to admit
that it took balls to drive three miles in traffic (they'd
    tried this one before)
pick up your mother, run over your dog and still think
that you got one hell of a deal

the runner

if you drink at all in the boys neighborhood
you know about the runner
from bar to bar day after day
maybe fifty, may seventy
no matter
tall, lean, weathered
always eating Snickers and sucking down Tokay
where he got the money and the stamina to keep up
    the pace
is one more mystery spinning around the corner
all day from morning open to late night when he
    vanished
the runner ate his candy bars and drank his wine
he knew all the words to all the Charlie Pride songs on
    the juke
and always had lots of quarters to run the machine
    and play those tunes
in the dark of afternoon bar time it was reassuring
    getting hammered
as the runner stood in front of the juke box drunk
singing along with Charlie
he did this for years and even made the wall at
    uptown Eddie's Club
the original not the fern bar yuppie phony
where drunks legendary and some dead (those with
    gold stars on the prints)
were nailed in black-and-white photographic truth to
    the wall
for the viewing enjoyment of well-healed patrons
for quite a while everyone noticed that the runner
was absent from the scene at the corner
one cold January night as the wind growled and the
    snow slashed
the boys sat in The Mint working over highballs

The Boys on the Corner

when someone came in and said he'd looked in
    Eddie's front window
and saw the runner's mug with a gold star on it
someday they'd all be hanging there
so they drank up and ordered another round

the game's the same

the cats said it would be easy
but they thought the game was played with whiskey
but the boys knew better, knew the tough truth
the con with the Cubs and all the rest of it comes
    down to money
the fun is standing in the middle of this long running
    tale
while a trio of bustouts killing time for free drinks
blasts some old Ellington out the door of The Turtle
horsehide on a windy spring day
children in grandparents dress
fools in pinstripe cloth
beer here, bleachers there
at the Pioneer League stadium three blocks away
they love the game when it's played by ancient rules
a buxom sweetie in a blue tank top says I'm confused
we all are announce the boys with lazy lecherous
    intent
where's Willie someone asks
she's the tall girl down front says Ms. Buxom
these things are easy
it's an old game, the façade is the joke
that's what they all believe and it works
makes some sense
remember Ernie and the laughs we used to have
was it old times or stupidity rising in a crazed
    situation
put in Brock someone yells
the game's a joke and the boys know it
but belief has never mattered
old women have young dreams and they love the
    game, too
spring makes an appearance, the game returns
an old friend is back

simple minded

quick greed grabs
some untrammeled ass
sweeping contours
honest openness
still clean wind
on a higher level
a natural buxomness
jiggles alongside
a wild untamed mind
been doing this
for a long time
probably do it some more
except there are
self-centered-absorbed
rapists on the near horizon
riding down brazenly
through distilled purity
destroying with deep thrusts
and explosive spurts
wild dies a slow death
black blood flows
into the red dust
another indecency
gotten away with

dead end

this guy is headed to oblivion
he's turned state's evidence
on a big coke gig near the boys' corner
a bunch of people want him dead now
weird people that look murderous straight
who don't fit the neighborhood
walk the pavement at all hours
trying to kill the fool
others trying to keep him going until court
to make the nothing time case
a real pathetic scene
all these sick cats chasing down
a perverted righteous dream
the guy guzzles JW Black
substitutes methadone for heroin
what's he care
dead is dead
he's already there
the trial day flashed on
and after testifying he went to prison
on a short time deal
he's out now, but nobody recognizes his existence
he's still a dead man
always was

dt blues

the haze is real, so is the room
madman spinning flirtations with death
awful confrontations with diseased truth
nothing is comfortable except pain
a twenty year stumble to this place
dreams gone crazy, loving turned violent
whiskey the only truth in a crooked scene
get out of the way cause he's coming through guns and
    all
some of the clowns thought they could help
the talk-sincerity old-time medicine show
cerebral circle jerks in a hot sweaty room
the haze is real, it killed someone who got him here
fixations replaced with placeboes
craziness still dances on an un-dug grave
yes it's real, just clearer now

an old friend

one of the boys had an old friend that he hadn't seen
    in years
there is no one reason for not having been in contact
they just grew apart – he to Florida – the boy to the
    corner
one day when the boy visited his old neighborhood he
    saw his friend's sister
she told him a younger brother had blown his head off
    with a rifle in the basement
she wasn't happy to see him and wouldn't tell him
    where to contact his friend
after a few minutes she warmed to the scene and told
    the boy that
his friend was out of his office right now
told him some other things, too
he'd apparently been arrested for a series of minor
    thefts
trying to make the day-to-day buster
barely beat going to jail and assigned to work for the
    mayor as penance
he's done quite well and now has a job there and is in
    complete charge of emergencies
he's out on one now she said
the mayor's limo has dead battery so my friend called
    a purple code alert
big doing's way down south
his sister told me one more thing about my friend
he has a long, full beard and horns
grow out of his head that curve full circle like a ram's
the boy thanked her for her time
but doesn't think that he'll be trying
to get in touch with him anymore

fight

unmistakable sound
bone on face flesh
whap, whap, thunk
man down bleeding when
skull cracks on concrete
from eyes, nose, ears
other kicks him
in the gut
with worn-out shoes
the boys watch and drink
and smoke before
turning back to talking
about the price of gas
they don't own a car
mortgage rates
even they laugh at this one
cost of Beam, cigarettes
fools running for office
guy on the ground scrambles to knees
stands up wobbling
like a skinny tree
in high wind
other guy smashes nose to flat pulp
kicks in groin
boxes ears
and down he goes again
out for the count
rifles passed out man's wallet
bunch of wrinkled, ragged ones
and a five
all this wealth is
shoved in pocket
of greasy pants

John Holt

one of the boys asks
"what's that all about?'
guy says with a leer
"son-of-a-bitch looked
at me weird"
and he saunters
off towards the
open door at Mickey's
time for a drink
pack of smokes
the boys look at each other
shrug and resume the talk
"damn Vipers can't win
Colson can't hit
a curve ball to save his ass"
squad cruises by
cop waves
one of the good ones
time for more wine
change gathered
a couple of bottles and some smokes
"Burguillos has no change-up
and no heat"
legless man on
skate board pulls up
using tape wrapped knuckles
for traction in
slippery world, slick times
to downed man
cradles his head
wraps tightly broken melon
with several winds
of duct tape
then wheels over
down around corner
whistling Strangers in the Night

The Boys on the Corner

on it goes
while the man on the pavement
groans and rolls over
in his blood and vomit

don't cry, it's only the edge

come on, give it a shot, it won't kill ya
let's see what your made of the boys say to a passerby
fears, joys, personal triumphs, fetishes
the whole works
sailing around alone you can lie your ass off
and isn't that a lot of fun
we've all tried that little diversion once or twice
give her a hug, tell her a secret, she's hip to vertigo
the paradoxical qualities of loneliness lend
a bit of topspin to the game
win or lose, it's always more fun as a player
watching is for the weak, the mental deficients
metaphysics aside, how many tunes does the band
    know?
you aren't one of those are you?
we've heard that one before, doesn't wash
vanished furniture, bad checks, murdered credit
disbelief, despair, isolation
these aren't glittering products
foisted on a starling market
the band does know that tune but they're drunk and
don't want to play it anymore
so lean way out over the edge
feel the wind blow as it tries to knock you off balance
one hell of a view isn't it
sure falling will bust you up some
maybe even kill you
but you're damn near dead anyway
take a chance, come on....

crazy pissed off

the man's nuts
always yelling about nothing
swearing
swinging stork arms
through the air
near anyone who
made the mistake
of coming too close
spastic karate kicks
that hit nothing
he'd been wealthy once
but drank up all of his money
after learning the wife
was screwing his
best friend
she finally left him for
the dear soul
the man went nuts
always drunk now
stoned on percocet, vicodin
any script he can score
yellow-eyed mad man stare
through the blood shot vision
always yelling about
bad women, no money
he'd say to anyone who'd listen
"I'm crazy pissed off"

About the Author

John Holt is the author of more than two dozen published books including, *Plain Crazy in Paradise, Blown Away Under the Big Sky, The Lost Patrol, Yellowstone Drift - Floating the Past in Real Time, Arctic Aurora - Canada's Yukon and Northwest Territories, Coyote Nowhere - In Search of America's Last Frontier.* Some of the poems in *The Boys on the Corner* originally appeared in slightly different form in publications that include *Plain Crazy in Paradise, High County News, The Azorean Express, Counterpunch.org* and *The Midwest Poetry Review.* His work has appeared in such publications as *Men's Journal, Fly Fisherman, Crossroads, The Denver Post* and *E - The Environmental Magazine.* He and his wife, photographer Ginny Holt, live in Livingston, Montana.

www.ingramcontent.com/pod-product-compliance
Lightning Source LLC
Chambersburg PA
CBHW072031170426

43200CB00025B/2504